RTY-
HT
NESSES

THIRTY-EIGHT WITNESSES

The Kitty Genovese Case

by
A.M. Rosenthal

University of California Press

Berkeley
Los Angeles
London

THIRTY-EIGHT WITNESSES:
THE KITTY GENOVESE CASE

University of California Press
Berkeley and Los Angeles, California

University of California Press, Ltd.
London, England
First University of California Press
Paperback, 1999

Library of Congress Cataloging-in-Publication Data
Rosenthal, A. M. (Abraham Michael), 1922–
  Thirty-eight witnesses : the Kitty Genovese case /
by A. M. Rosenthal.
       p.   cm.
  Originally published: [1st ed.] New York :
     McGraw-Hill, [1964]
  ISBN: 0-520-21527-3 (alk. paper)
    1. Murder—New York (State)—New York.   2.
Genovese, Catherine, d. 1964.   3. Police—New York
(State)—New York.   4. Witnesses—New York (State)—
New York.   5. Telephone—United States—Emergency
reporting systems.   6. Apathy.   7. Responsibility.
8. Social ethics.   I. Title.   II. Title: 38 witnesses

HV6534.N5 R65 1999
364.15'23'09747243—dc21   98-3431
                                                         CIP

Photographs courtesy of
The New York Times.

Acknowledgment

This edition of *Thirty-Eight Witnesses* was inspired by Andrew Blauner, the literary agent of New York. For years he has had an intense interest in the story of Catherine Genovese and was determined that my original version of *Thirty-Eight Witnesses* be reprinted and updated.

INTRODUCTION

to Paperback Edition

Soon after I returned from years of reporting in far places and was beginning my work as a newspaper editor in New York City, I wrote a small book about a woman called Catherine Genovese.

I had never met her or anybody who had known her. I knew very little about her except that she was twenty-eight years old when I first heard her name, that she was an Italian American with a thin, serious face and worked tending bar in a middle-class neighborhood in the borough of Queens. Her parents were unhappy that she lived alone. They wanted her to live with them in their house in a suburb of New York City.

That was thirty-four years ago, as I write. Even now, I do not know a great deal more about her life. Her life was not the reason that I wrote about her, or that millions of people came to know her name and have never forgotten it, and that for more than three decades she has affected my life and work, which for most journalists are pretty much the same thing.

I was interested only in the manner of her dying. She died in the early hours of March 13, 1964, outside the small apartment house in Queens where she lived, as neighbors heard her scream her last half hour away and did nothing, nothing at all, to give her succor or even cry alarm.

Her death, not her life, has been written about all these years since it took place. It has been the subject of lectures and seminars in universities, of sermons in churches and synagogues, of several television dramas, and of at least ten plays. One opened in Los Angeles and another in Buenos Aires; other writers are working still on the story of Catherine Genovese. I know because they write to me. They seek some new insight from me, and I from them. We keep seeking, so strong is the memory of Catherine Genovese—the memory, that is, of the way of her dying.

Her name, once known only to her family and the people she served at the bar, has taken on instantly understood meaning to all who have heard it. The Kitty Genovese story, the Genovese case, has become both a quick, puffy cliché for apathy and cowardice about the suffering of others, and an intellectual and religious puzzlement: what does it mean to me?

To me, you, we. That is the power of the Genovese matter. It talks to us not about her, a subject that was barely of fleeting interest to us, but about ourselves, a subject never out of our minds.

Nor do we think much about the man who stabbed her to death and then lay down on her body to ejaculate. Even the neighbors who heard her scream and cry for life, who never walked down the stairs to help or even called the police, are not thought of as individuals but as a clump—the thirty-eight witnesses, we call them and always will—not this one and that one and the other, but the clump. The words mean callousness and cowardice beyond our comprehension; we say that.

The witnesses have not told us much about themselves. Why should they? Go away, get the hell away from my door, they told reporters. We know that they were perfectly ordinary people, skilled workers, tradesmen, people making a living, not bothering anybody, never known to be cruel or cowardly. If we did know more about some of them, would it tell us what we wanted to know, and was that the reason we will not allow the death of Catherine Genovese to escape us? I do not think so.

In the first days after I was involved in the Genovese case, I thought the question and answer were simple. Would I have helped her, at least picked up the phone, for heaven's sake? All my friends and I were sure we would.

By the time I began the little book about her, I was making the questions a little harder on myself. Like the thirty-eight witnesses, had I ever turned away from a person who was in desperate need and whom I could have helped at no risk to myself? Yes, I had and said so with some satisfaction at being so candid and self-examining.

Years later I understood that neither I nor my friends had been giving the answers to more important questions, had never been willing even to pose them to ourselves. But I think we must have known these questions all the time, because they involved the way of the world, which was not acceptable, if we had to think about it.

In the years that have passed since her death, we have learned something, not much, about Catherine Genovese. I feel it impudently familiar to call her Kitty, which the papers always do; she died too hard and we do not know her well enough and never will.

We know that she worked at the bar at night, which the family, parents, brothers, and sister, did not like. Certainly if she had worked days, Winston Moseley would never have seen her when he was out in the early morning hours of March 13, 1964, hunting.

When the report of the murder of a woman on Austin Street came into the *Times* later the day she died, the *Times* gave it about the same amount of attention as it gave any murder in Queens those days—about four paragraphs. I was not even aware of the story; it was not important enough for my attention as metropolitan editor. An assistant handled that kind of thing and made the appropriate sign to a rewrite man: thumb and forefinger held up, a small space between them that meant keep it short.

I was trying to rediscover New York, where I had been brought up. I had returned less than seven months earlier. Physically, I had been away from New York City for about ten years. I spent that decade abroad as a foreign correspondent for the *Times,* first covering India, Pakistan, Afghanistan, Nepal, and Ceylon from my base in New Delhi, occasionally being assigned to Vietnam, Malaysia, or New Guinea. Somebody on the foreign desk at the *Times* thought New Guinea must be near India—out there someplace.

I wrote mostly about India for four years. In 1958

I was sent to Poland to cover what was then Communist Eastern Europe. When the local dictator decided he had had enough of me and ordered me out after less than two years in Warsaw, I spent another two years in Western Europe and Africa. Then, back to Asia, for two more based in Japan.

Journalistically, I had been away eight years longer. Before going abroad I had lived in New York but had been assigned to cover the brand-new United Nations. My life had revolved around U.N. news, and many of my friends were U.N. delegates or members of the international secretariat.

So when the paper asked me to return from Japan to New York and become metropolitan editor, I did not relish the idea at all. The Khyber Pass was my kind of story, I said, not the Bronx. But New York wanted to try me out as an editor and I submitted, figuring that after two or three years I would either get the London bureau as the reward for my sacrifice or run off again to India, India, India. It did not work out that way. I remained an editor, but always in my mind still king of the Khyber Pass.

In New York I set about doing what I would have done in any new foreign assignment: find out who ran the place and get to know them. I knew that had not been done much at the *Times,* where editors then stayed in the office as the receptacle for reporters' ideas. But I was sure that the reporters would love the change—the editor, still in his heart a reporter like them, getting off his chair, getting to know the city, coming back with ideas himself. Wouldn't that be great for everybody? They hated it, of course—didn't I trust them, poking around their assignments?

Among the people I got to know was the police commissioner. One day at lunch near City Hall, when we were talking about police problems, he told me about neighbors who had not come to the help of a dying young woman. I said it sounded like a good story, which surprised him a little, the *Times* not being known as a great crime newspaper. The *Times'*s story about her death and the neighbors who heard her scream but did not help or call for help was picked up by the print and broadcast press around the world as a stunning example of apathy—other people's apathy.

When I wrote the book, I did not know much about Winston Moseley either. I knew from the arrest record that he was going on thirty and made a good living as a technician on calculating machines. He supported his wife and children, a quiet, very neat man.

We could have learned a great deal more about Moseley at the trial, and about Catherine Genovese's death. But the trial did not get much attention. The details were not the kind of material the *Times* or most other papers printed then or now.

I read the trial transcript through before writing this introduction to a new edition of the book. I knew it would be an unspeakable insult to Catherine Genovese for me to write about her again and walk away from the record of her death, which was her last scream.

Winston Moseley talked at great length and with entire calm about what he liked most to do. He liked to go out in the streets in the early mornings to rob men or kill women. If he spotted a man who was not too large, and was walking carelessly, or weaving, he enjoyed robbing him with a gun or at knifepoint and taking his money. He did not need money, but taking it away from a man he could catch off guard and overpower with a weapon gave him pleasure.

But it was not nearly as enjoyable as hunting women. He was black, a fact we did not print after he was arrested. Some white readers sent us nasty letters about that. *Times* policy is not to print that infor-

mation in crime stories unless it is specifically pertinent to the crime or part of the description when police search for a wanted person.

Moseley did not care whether the women he hunted were black or white, except once, when he made the choice out of curiosity. Often he did not know. He never saw them clearly until they turned to face him, with his knife deep in them or his gun in their back. Sometimes he did not see them until they stared up at him from the ground, or he had to turn them over to see what they looked like.

What he looked for was a woman alone, walking or driving a car. If she was driving, he followed her in his car, and when she stopped, he stopped too and parked. Then he got out to track her on foot for the kill.

He says he did that at least five times and confessed to killing two other women before Catherine Genovese walked toward her home that night in March. Police say his confession about the first murder, of a woman called Barbara Kralik, was made because he knew he would be convicted in the Genovese case and was trying to help a friend who had confessed to the Kralik murder.

But about the murder of Anna May Johnson, everything he said checked out. She was not important in the Genovese case except as verification of his modus operandi. But I want to write a bit about her death. When someday I read this remembrance of the Genovese case in print, I do not want to have to ask myself why I turned away from another murdered woman because she was no great news story, not even worth the four paragraphs Catherine Genovese was awarded the day after her death.

Anna May Johnson was killed about 2 A.M. on February 28, 1964. Moseley testified in the Genovese case that he saw Anna May Johnson in her car. He followed it to near her small apartment house in South Ozone Park, Queens. When she got out, he followed on foot. She turned and saw him behind her. He asked for money and she gave it to him.

"Then I shot her. . . . I shot her in the stomach."

He shot her again, then "I turned her over and then I could see for sure that she was dead. Then I decided, well, perhaps I'd rape her now that she was dead so I took off all her clothes that she had, right there in the snow. . . . Then I decided it was too cold out in the snow so I rolled her up the steps on into the house into the middle of the living room floor. . . . So first of all I committed that cunnilingus, was it? But I was impotent . . . I laid on top of her. . . . I did have an orgasm."

After that, he dragged her upstairs to her apartment.

"I set a fire in two places in the living room and I took the scarf that she had on and put that on the lower part of her body . . . on her genital organs and set fire to her." The next morning he went to work.

Winston Moseley went hunting again two weeks later and saw Catherine Genovese driving alone in a red car. He was picked up six days after her death. He was picked up because he was suspected of robberies, police say. Under some "persuasive" questioning, as he put it, he told them not only about the robberies but confirmed their suspicions that he was the killer of Catherine Genovese. He went to trial on June 8, 1964.

The defense did not challenge the confession but asked for acquittal on grounds of insanity. These are excerpts from testimony under questioning by his own lawyer.

Q: Now, on this night did you intend killing?

A: Yes.

Q: What if anything did you do to prepare for that?

A: Well, I had a hunting knife that I had taken from a previous burglary, and I took that with me.

Q: Had you any specific type of individual in mind?

A: Well, I knew it would be a woman.

Q: Is there any reason why now you intended to kill a white woman as distinguished from the two prior times that you thought you killed colored?

A: No, unless perhaps I might have been thinking there might have been some difference between them.

Q: Now tell us what you did, please.

A: Well, I left the house about one-thirty or two o'clock, and it took me until about three o'clock to find one that was driving where I could actually catch up with her. . . . I followed [her red car] for about ten blocks, and then it pulled into what I thought was a parking lot.

Q: Did you make your mind up to kill her?

A: Yes.

Q: Can you tell us any reasons why?

A: No, I can't give you any reasons why.

The court: Was [money] one of the factors?

A: It possibly was, but it was not a primary factor.

xviii Q: You tell us exactly what happened, Winston.

A: As soon as she got out of the car she saw me and ran. I ran after her and I had a knife in my hand, then I caught up with her and I stabbed her twice in the back.

He testified that he stabbed her in the chest and stomach as well as the back, that somebody called out the window, but that he "did not think that person would come down to help her."

Moseley also testified that later he had heard somebody open an apartment door and shout down, but he "didn't feel these people" were coming down the stairs. So he lifted her skirt, cut off her underclothes, including her brassiere.

After he had stabbed her repeatedly he began to worry that somebody might have seen his car and noted the color, make, or license. So he walked back to the outdoor parking lot where he had left it to stalk her on foot. He moved the car around the corner. Then he took off his hat, a stocking cap, and put on a fedora he had in the car.

Q: [*from the prosecutor*] Why?

A: Well, I felt that perhaps if I had not killed the

girl and had to leave what I started unfinished, she would have only seen the bottom half of my face.

Q: In other words, you thought you could disguise your face better by putting on a different hat.

A: That's right.

Q: Now, when you came back, you were thinking, weren't you, about what you were going to do?

A: That's right.

Q: What?

A: That's right.

Moseley said he heard some yelling from windows, but it had stopped by the time he got back to Catherine Genovese, whom he had left lying in the street. He did not think that anybody would come down "regardless to the fact that she had screamed."

"So I came back but I didn't see her. . . . I tried the first door in the row of those back houses, which was locked. The second door was open and she was in there. As soon as she saw me she started screaming so I stabbed her a few other times . . . once in the neck. . . . She only moaned after that."

Q: You also knew that people at three o'clock in
   the morning on a cold morning would not take
   the trouble to even come down and investigate
   if someone had been killed?

A: I thought that way, yes.

Q: And as she started to scream, you stabbed her,
   didn't you?

A: Yes, I did.

Q: You stabbed her in the throat?

A: Right.

Q: That is where the voice was coming from, isn't
   that right?

A: That's right.

Moseley testified that he saw that she was
exposed, decided to rape her, stabbed her again, that
she kept moaning, that he took off one of his gloves
to pull down his zipper, took out his penis, laid on top
of her but could not attain—"What was the word?"
he asked the judge. "Erection," said the court.

   Did he have an orgasm, the court asked. Moseley said yes. He also said she was menstruating at the
time. He took the money from her wallet.

Q: Forty-nine dollars you put in your pocket, hah?

A: That's being practical.

Q: Being practical?

A: Yes. Why would I throw money away?

He left. Somebody then did call the police. A half hour had gone by in the two attacks on Catherine Genovese, what with seventeen stabbings, Moseley's back and forth from the parking lot, cutting her clothes off, raping her, and so on. She died soon after arrival in the hospital. If the call had come more quickly, the police said later, her life could have been saved.

Moseley said he did not know for sure that she was dead until he read it in the newspapers the next day. He committed at least three robberies between the time of the murder and the day the police arrested him.

The trial took three days. He was convicted and sentenced to death. Later an appeals court found that the trial judge had not allowed sufficient testimony about Moseley's life in the sentencing hearings and therefore commuted the death sentence to life.

Four years later he cut himself with a bottle at the state prison in Attica, was sent to a prison hospital in Buffalo, and escaped by overpowering a guard. In the next four days, according to the police, he raped a woman, beat her husband, fled in their car, took two men and a woman hostage, and surrendered after a face-off with the Federal Bureau of Investigation.

In prison, Moseley began taking courses that earned him a college degree. That got him some print in newspapers. He wrote letters to newspapers saying he was a different man and deserved another chance to become part of society. In 1977, the *Times* printed an Op-Ed piece from him, explaining why he should be freed to become an "asset to society."

In the 1980s Moseley began asking for parole, which he did not get.

In 1995, thirty-one years after her death, he appealed for a new trial on the grounds that he had not had an appropriate, objective defense, since he said he had recently discovered that his lawyer had once represented Catherine Genovese when she got a ticket for gambling. Catherine Genovese's three brothers and sister had not attended the murder trial but appeared at the hearings. One brother, William, had lost both legs above the knee in Vietnam and hoisted himself onto a front bench from his wheelchair.

The original lawyer for Moseley testified that

before the trial he had told Moseley about his earlier representation of Catherine Genovese. The judge called the representation "ephemeral" and said it created no bias in the lawyer against his client Moseley. The appeal was rejected. Winston Moseley is still in prison, planning another appeal to become a social asset.

For months after Catherine Genovese's death, newspapers, magazines, and TV shows ran stories and analyses by psychologists and academics as to how it could have happened: a girl dying screaming while thirty-eight neighbors heard, never came down, did not pick up a phone to call the police. Some letters to the editor denounced the silent witnesses. Other letters and some of the specialists, then and since, have tried to explain them.

Screaming at night—how could they be sure it was not a fight between husband and wife, lover and lover. Any fool knows that is the kind of thing where the rage and violence turn on the interloper who gets between them; first thing you know, the jerk gets hurt.

Yes, they should have called the police. But as the *Times* and other papers explained, other cities had far more convenient systems of calling the police (New York did not yet have the 911 system) that guaranteed anonymity. Some specialists blamed TV violence for instilling terror, or urban detachment from neighbors and, more frequently, "fear of the street," the fear of getting involved in something beyond their control.

Even if they just called the police, would they have to go to the police station, give evidence, and maybe testify in court? Maybe the thirty-eight witnesses worried about that, and can you really blame them entirely?

People in New York, around the country, and then in the seminars asked themselves whether they would ever refuse to give help to a person they could hear calling for help, just put themselves to a little trouble when there was no chance of real danger or cost? They thought they would not refuse under those conditions.

As I was writing *Thirty-Eight Witnesses,* I felt the question should be reworded so: would I ever refuse *again*?

I knew most of us had refused in the past, so often that we had become unaware of what we were doing.

I have walked past lepers and beggars scores of times in Asia. Any help from me, the merest, would have been of importance to them. They were terribly

sick; I saw their sores. If they were professional beggars, as I told myself, did that salve their sores or
straighten the limbs of the twisted children they held
up, rented or not?

With a few pennies I could have helped them,
but then others would have come up, crowded around,
and *touched* me, and I could not stand the thought of
that. So I walked away when the cost of helping them
would have been less than the cost of a phone call
for the thirty-eight, and no danger of being stabbed
or involved.

Cripples crawling in New Delhi's Connaught
Place, the capital's shopping center then, wretched
misshapen babies held out by filthy mothers in
Calcutta—I turned away not in fear but in disgust and
annoyance.

Certainly those emotions are less worthy than fear
as excuses for refusing succor, particularly as excuses
to oneself if encountered in an honest moment.

But the mystery for all of us about the Genovese
case was how could it have happened that thirty-eight
people, thirty-eight, heard the screams and did nothing. Two or three, all right, maybe even a half dozen—
it could happen. But everybody, all thirty-eight of
them?

I was trying hard to be candid with myself, but not hard enough. Now and for some years I have realized that I failed to ask the question that might have answered the mystery of so many silent witnesses on Austin Street.

Who was walking with me on that street in Calcutta or New Delhi and not stopping to give help? Not thirty-eight people, but hundreds at any one moment, thousands in an hour.

In the middle of a cold night, thirty-eight people refused the risk of being stabbed or getting involved by answering a cry for help of a person they could not see. Is that a greater mystery, a greater offense, than that by light of day thousands on a single street withhold help to suffering people, when it would cost them virtually nothing and put them in no peril, even though they see their faces and sores?

Are the people who turned away that one night in Queens, each in a separate decision, any more immoral or indecent or cowardly because there happened to be thirty-eight, than if there were just one of them? Does God judge by the individual or by head count?

And what if we hear the scream but cannot see the screamer? Of all questions about silent witnesses, to me this is the most important.

Suppose the screamer is not downstairs but around the corner. Surely somebody else is closer, so we don't have to run out, do we? What is the accepted distance for hearing but not moving—two flights down, five, one block, two blocks, three?

Suppose you know people screaming under persecution—not discrimination but persecution, as in imprisonment, torture, cells—for their politics or their religion. You have seen the smuggled pictures of bodies after the rack, you have heard from those who have escaped: your own government reports their existence in the Chinese gulag, the Laogai. You know they scream, but they are not within sight and you cannot reach out and touch them, nor are you allowed to visit them. But the screams are piercing.

How far away do you have to be to forgive yourself for not doing whatever is in your power to do: stop doing business with the torturer, or just speak up for them, write a letter, join a human rights group, go to church and pray for the rescue of the persecuted and the damnation of the persecutors, give money, do something.

Three stories up, a thousand miles, ten thousand miles, from here to Austin Street, or from here to the gulags or the dungeons for political and religious prisoners anywhere? How far is silence from a place of safety acceptable without detesting yourself as we detest the thirty-eight? Tell me, what question is more important than the one Catherine Genovese put to me for years when I sat down to write my columns for the *Times*—how far?

INTRODUCTION

by
Arthur Ochs Sulzberger

A newspaper is print and ink, and many things. There is no counting the hours that we who work on *The New York Times* have spent, and still spend, analyzing, assessing, diagnosing our own paper, our relationship to it and what it means to our readers.

Some things are known but unsaid. More than print and ink, a newspaper is a collection of fierce individualists who somehow manage to perform the astounding daily miracle of merging their own personalities under the discipline of the deadline, and retain the flavor of their own minds in print. In dread fear of sentimentality, another thing true is not said—that for its staff the paper is a source of pride and, I do believe, an object of affection and—yes, love.

Looking outward, we know and relish the knowledge that *The Times* has come to be regarded as a newspaper that pays minute attention to all matters of foreign and national significance. In a news sense we are an international and national newspaper.

But that is not all we are. It is often forgotten—I think sometimes by ourselves—that we are above all a community newspaper. We print for a specific community and although we search for readership beyond it, that community is our bread and butter, and its members the real basis of our existence.

We are *The New York Times,* not the *Times* of London or of Los Angeles or of Washington. Our readers are people who live in the city or its suburbs and although they are interested in foreign and national affairs they are quite as interested, perhaps more, in what takes place in the City Council as in the Security Council. Sometimes we suffer from Afghanistanitis—the theory that what happens in exotic places is somehow more important than what happens in Queens. But by and large, and more and more, we hold to the realization that metropolitan news is the essential third leg of our stool.

When we forget it, the reaction of our readers to what is taking place in their own home town reminds us. The experts may write us letters after a story about India or the Soviet Union. The non-experts, the people for whom we publish, write to us about New York. And they care, deeply.

Every now and then, a story comes along that

stirs our city, makes it think and makes it talk. There have not been many that have moved the city more than the story told in this book, the story of the thirty-eight witnesses. It tells something about our city, but more important, it tells something about each one of us.

Arthur Ochs Sulzberger
President and Publisher
The New York Times

PART ONE

This small book is about a woman I never met but who touched my life as she did the lives of many other people—some tens of thousands, I think. I know very little about her except her name, which was Catherine Genovese, and her age, which was twenty-eight, and the manner of her dying.

It is also about thirty-eight of her neighbors, about whom all I know is that they are much like other people of decent middle-class background. The only thing that distinguishes them and, I believe, now harrows their lives a bit, is that on the night of March 13, 1964, each one of them turned away from a cry in the night.

A great many hard things have been said about these thirty-eight, and I am sure they are bewildered, and I know they are resentful. But it is important to say this—that what they did happens every night, in every city. The terror of the story of Catherine Genovese is simply that by happenstance all thirty-eight did that night what each one alone might have done any night without the city having known, or cared. In my own mind, and I believe in the minds of others, this has presented a question that troubles and will not recede: is the ugliness in the number or is it in the act itself, and are thirty-eight sins truly more important than one?

This small book is about a number of connected things—an anecdote told in passing by a commissioner of police who looks like a tough Irish cop because he is a tough Irish cop but who also happens to be a man of knowledge and sensitivity; a newspaper story; a few sociologists; a most cautious theologian; and how so many good people try so desperately to make collective their individual guilt.

At the end of this book are set down some of my thoughts on the meaning of the death of Catherine Genovese. But in some embarrassment I say now that these are not meant as a sermon. I say this in the haunting fear of being told—by myself, mostly—to practice what is preached and because I know I cannot. All I believe, and this most fervently, is that a truth remains a truth whether or not a man has the strength to follow it.

The first time the name of Catherine Genovese appeared in *The New York Times* was on March 14,

2

1964—a four-paragraph story. The heading, small type given to stories of minor importance usually printed simply for the record, read: "Queens Woman Is Stabbed to Death in Front of Home."

Catherine Genovese

The story written by a young police reporter read:

"A twenty-eight-year-old Queens woman was stabbed to death early yesterday morning outside her apartment house in Kew Gardens.

"Neighbors who were awakened by her screams found the woman, Miss Catherine Genovese of 82-70 Austin Street, shortly after 3 A.M. in front of a building three doors from her home.

"The police said that Miss Genovese had been attacked in front of her building and had run to

3

where she fell. She had parked her car in a nearby lot, the police said, after having driven it from the Hollis bar where she was day manager.

"The police, who spent the day searching for the murder weapon, interviewing witnesses and checking automobiles that had been seen in the neighborhood, said last night that they had no clues."

Other newspapers carried roughly the same kind of story.

On *The Times,* I am the Metropolitan Editor, a job that used to go by the name of City Editor, and which is still a little difficult for most newspapermen to get their tongues around. I head a staff of about 200 reporters and editors responsible for covering the city, its huge suburbs, and a couple of neighboring states.

It is a rather strange job and I still am coming slowly to understand it, and sometimes feel like a small boy just learning to read, taking up a storybook and searching for letters and short words that give him clues to the story. It is strange for me perhaps because eighteen of the twenty years I have spent on *The Times* have been devoted to diplomatic or foreign reporting, and to a certain extent I grew away from the city that was my home. For almost a decade, reality to myself, my wife and our three sons was not the Grand Concourse in the Bronx or Broadway in Manhattan but Nizamuddin in New Delhi or Chodkiewicze Street in Warsaw.

Quite suddenly, the focus of life shifted—for my boys to a public school on the East Side of Manhattan, for myself to a great city I thought I no longer knew, but which I found more a part of myself and my half-hidden memories than I had ever realized. I found myself missing the liberty I had abroad, but so enveloped by the pace and excitement of New York and fascinated by the always elusive goal of trying to figure out a way of pinning down the city in newsprint that past freedoms lost some of their poignancy. The essence of New York still eludes me, as it does all newspapermen—is it pace or is it mixture, is it grayness or is it brightness, is it power or is it the diffusion of power, is it sophistication or is it vulgarity? But it seems enormously worth chasing, somehow. Journalistically, is New York a front-page story or is it a four-paragraph story?

I have no recollection whatever of that four-paragraph story being assigned or written. Early in the job I had come to the delightful rationalization that I could not occupy myself with every little story that came in during the course of the day, and that the price of sanity was selectivity combined, hopefully, with newspaper intuition. If the story had been reported to me, I would have ordered, I think, quite exactly the kind of story that did appear—a brief newspaper follow-up of the police blotter.

The truth also is that if Miss Genovese had been killed on Park Avenue or Madison Avenue an assistant would have called the story to my attention, I would have assigned a top man, and quite possibly we would have had a front-page story the next morning. If she had been a white woman killed in Harlem, the tension of the integration story would have provided her with a larger obituary. If she had been a Negro killed in Harlem she would have received a paragraph or two.

In twenty years in the newspaper business, I have spent only four nights covering police news, but I remember quite distinctly a police reporter of some experience telling me then of the relationship of color and geography to crime news—"Above 125th Street, if there's a killing don't bother phoning the desk; it happens too often."

Quite naturally, I pride myself on being a different breed of newspaperman than that old police reporter—traveled and socially conscious. I can find no philosophic excuse for giving the murder of a middle-class Queens woman less attention than the murder of a Park Avenue broker but journalistically no apologies are offered—news is not philosophy or theology but what certain human beings, reporters and editors, know will have meaning and interest to other human beings, readers. Within that definition there is range for almost anything that can befall man or mankind. How much attention it gets still depends largely on where it befalls, and to whom.

Death took Miss Genovese in Queens, a borough of New York growing faster than any other place in the city, home for 1.8 million people, most of whom are like most reporters and editors, not particularly poor, not particularly rich, not particularly famous. It is probably the least exotic place in the city— great housing developments crowding out the private homes that were once the borough's pride, a place of shopping centers and baby carriages and sewer troubles and, to newspapermen, paralyzing ordinariness.

The New York Times, which has full-time staff correspondents in Karachi and Stockholm and Léopoldville and Algiers, has no full-time reporter in Queens. It can be shown statistically, I believe, that in the past few years *Times* reporters have spent more time in Antarctica than in Queens. It is one of those places about which editors keep telling themselves that they really should get around to covering it someday, with a good young reporter; you know, a bright kid ready to climb.

So Catherine Genovese died in Queens and I assume I read the story in the paper the next day. I do not remember. I do remember that the first time her story came directly into my consciousness it was with a sense of irritation and professional annoyance.

We had carried a brief story the third week in March saying that a man called Winston Moseley, a twenty-nine-year-old business-machine operator, had been arrested for the murder of Miss Genovese, that police said he had confessed and that they said he had confessed to the killing of another Queens woman, Mrs. Annie May Johnson, a twenty-four-year-old housewife stabbed to death outside her house in Ozone Park, Queens, on February 29. (During the life of the story we received a few nasty letters demanding to know why we had "concealed" the fact that Moseley was a Negro. The answer is really quite simple. Where the fact that a man is a Negro is directly relevant to the story we print the fact. Where it is not, we do not.)

What irritated and annoyed me was a story a few days later in the New York *Daily News* that Moseley had also confessed to the murder of a fifteen-year-old girl, Barbara Kralik, in July 1963, and that the police were holding another man from whom they had had a confession, and that this situation embarrassed officialdom no end. I was upset not for any moral reason at all but simply because we had not had the story ourselves. The double confession in the Kralik case, incidentally, has not been explained at the time of this writing.

The next Monday was the twenty-third of March and scrawled in the appointment book one of my sons had bought for me for Christmas was "lunch Murphy."

Michael Joseph Murphy is the Police Commissioner of New York, and I had lunched with him two or three times before, always at the same place—Emil's near City Hall. It is a good sauerbrauten and dumpling place full of politicians and city officials who mind their own business and don't table-hop.

The Commissioner always has the same table toward the middle of the restaurant, sits always with his back to the wall, an old police habit, and orders shrimp curry and rice in the touching belief that the dish is somehow non-caloric.

There was nothing particularly strange or unusual about my meetings with Murphy. I was new to the city after a decade abroad, and, I wanted to get to know him as I wanted to get to know the Housing Commissioner or the Mayor or judges or playwrights or bankers or anybody else who has anything significant to do with the life of the city. We talked off the record, but I wasn't after secrets and he wasn't after telling me any. I wanted simply to form my own impressions of a man important in the news of New York.

Murphy did not have a murder on his mind that day; he rarely does. In the spring of 1964, what was usually on the mind of the Police Commissioner of New York—as it was of most policemen and politicians—was the haunting fear that someday blood would flow in the streets of New York because of the tensions of the civil rights movement. He lives with fear of a fire from a match carelessly or deliberately thrown away igniting in the ready, dry

10

kindling wood of Harlem. His talk was of integration movements and civil rights and civil rights leaders and civil rights laws, not of detectives and precincts and stabbings. He is six feet tall and weighs 200 pounds and came up through the ranks and is a cop's cop, but he is also the holder of three degrees, all of them earned while working policeman's hours. He is neither a great hero nor a great leader, but he is intelligent and he is tough and he runs his own department.

I had a question in my mind that day, and just before coffee I asked it. I did not remember the names involved. I was not really interested in the women murdered or the details of their deaths, but that one man had confessed to a murder for which the police were already holding another. I also remember thinking that this story would do the Queens District Attorney, Frank O'Connor, no particular good in his enthusiastic quest for the Governorship.

"What about that double confession out in Queens?" I asked Murphy. "What's that story all about, anyway?"

Now, early in my newspaper career I encountered the stunning reality that a policeman does not have to answer a reporter's questions. This truth broke upon me when I had been a reporter for about four days. I was sent out to cover a suicide at a "good address"—a Park Avenue hotel. I knew exactly what to do. I marched into the hotel, asked the elevator man where the trouble was, took the elevator up, knocked on the door.

A detective twelve feet tall opened the door, and I started to walk forward, where I was introduced to his hand, about three feet wide, held up before my face.

"Where are you going, kid?" he asked.

"There's a suicide here."

"So?"

"Reporter. I want to come in and talk to you and see the body."

"Beat it."

Beat it? I wasn't quite sure of the follow-through.

"But I am from *The Times,* a reporter."

"So?"

"Don't you care if I get the story right?" I asked righteously and indignantly.

"Four eyes," said the detective, amiably, "I don't care if you drop dead." Then he introduced me to the closed door. Thus I learned that, contrary to what I had believed as an article of faith, it was not the ordained, patriotic duty of every American to answer every reporter's every question.

At Emil's, the Police Commissioner did not tell me he did not care if I ceased suddenly to exist. But he looked at me from the corner of his eye, and said he knew nothing about the double confession. Somehow, I feel still that he was being less than utterly frank with me.

After a moment the Commissioner half turned toward me.

"That Queens story is something else," he said. "Remember we talked about apathy, public apathy toward law enforcement?"

We had, several times. The Commissioner had said what every cop often says—that one of the troubles with New York was that people didn't give a damn, wanted to stay out of trouble, wouldn't co-operate. An old cop complaint, nothing very new in it.

"Brother," the Commissioner said, "that Queens story is one for the books."

Thirty-eight people, the Commissioner said, had watched a woman being killed in the "Queens story" and not one of them had called the police to save her life.

"Thirty-eight?" I asked.

13

And he said, "Yes, thirty-eight. I've been in this business a long time, but this beats everything."

I experienced then that most familiar of newspapermen's reaction—vicarious shock. This is a kind of professional detachment that is the essence of the trade—the realization that what you are seeing or hearing will startle a reader. The reporter or the editor need not, and usually is not, shocked or startled himself but he experiences the flashing realization that readers will be.

I told the Commissioner that this seemed to be a story, and since our talk was entirely off the record up to then, asked his agreement to my assigning a reporter to look into it. He agreed.

I rode back to 43rd Street in a police car, and was a little disappointed that nobody saw me drive up. In the newsroom, I was caught up as usual like a shirt in a laundry machine by the news of the day, and forgot the whole thing until about 5 P.M. when it popped back in my mind.

I was sure that the Commissioner had been exaggerating, but the story was clearly worth looking into. People doing nothing about a murder—even if there were only eight or nine or so—was

14

obviously a story. Thirty-eight was impossible, I knew.

I asked an assistant to call Marty Gansberg over the loudspeaker. (Our newsroom is so large we need a public-address system, but it seems terribly impersonal to me, and I soothe my sense of outrage in summoning a reporter mechanically by getting somebody else to do it.)

Gansberg is an old hand at *The Times* but new at reporting; he had been a copy editor and wanted to try his hand at something different. For weeks afterward, a variety of reporters asked me—more in anger than in sorrow—why I had chosen somebody so new and not experienced reporters such as themselves, for instance.

The reasons were: (a) Gansberg has a sense of enthusiasm, and I knew I wouldn't have to sell him on the story; (b) he is new enough not to resent dogged difficult work that might turn to nothing, as this story might have turned out; and (c) he was within my line of vision.

Eighteen years ago, I happened to be within the line of vision of Turner Catledge, then Assistant Managing Editor of *The Times,* when he wanted a   **15** kid with good legs to trail Andrei Gromyko around town, and that is how I became a diplomatic reporter and then a foreign correspondent. This priceless bit of know-how has been locked within my professional bosom ever since.

Gansberg came up. Looking back now, he says firmly that I told him what I knew, and said, "Gansberg, get that story!" An entrancing thought; I wish I had the personality to go with it. "Get that story, Gansberg!" "I want you to break the case by edition time, Gansberg!" "Gansberg, get out there and come back with a scoop!" I've tried out a variety of ringing commands to myself since Gansberg told me that, but they just don't come off. What I said, I think, was, "Marty, would you mind taking a look at this thing?"

When I was talking to Marty, I realized that I was not sure whether the Commissioner had been talking about the Genovese murder or the others in Queens.

Gansberg went back to his desk in the dim recesses of the newsroom, and called District Attorney O'Connor. Gansberg asked the District Attorney about the double confession in the Kralik case. O'Connor said he was sure that the first man

16

arrested had killed Barbara Kralik, not Moseley. But what Gansberg was after was the story of the witnesses, and O'Connor told him that he must be thinking of the Genovese murder. O'Connor thought that there had been silent witnesses to that.

In Gansberg and myself, I think, a sense of excitement that is the reward of the business of newspapering kept growing. But still not large enough to keep me from pulling Gansberg off the story between phone calls to do other work. That night, Gansberg thought a lot about the Genovese story; even skipped Mitch Miller on TV to keep on thinking in the line of duty. The next morning he came in early and tried to set up an appointment in Queens with Assistant Chief Inspector Frederick M. Lussen.

It was not until Wednesday that Gansberg was able to reach Lussen. As he talked with Gansberg, Lussen received a call from headquarters informing him that he had just been promoted.

"This information induced him to smile," Gansberg says. "It was the only smile I saw on his face that afternoon. The man was angry with what he had to tell me. He was angry with the people."

Gansberg talked with every other detective on the case. They were angry too, as angry as detectives **17** allow themselves to get. Everybody said the same thing—thirty-eight witnesses, all silent during a murder—and every detective asked the same question: Why?

In the car to Kew Gardens, the detectives, as if mesmerized by the shock of the familiar become unrecognizable, kept saying what a nice neighborhood it was, how quiet, how respectable.

Gansberg seemed impressed by the number of trees, which to him seemed to be a sign of solidity. "The trees were bare, but there were so many of them, sycamores, Norway maples, silver maples, that you knew a good class of people lived around them," he says.

"There were some foreign accents to be heard in the streets and shops, because John F. Kennedy International Airport was nearby and many of the people in the neighborhood worked at the terminal.

"The more I walked around the neighborhood," Gansberg says, "the more I felt I wouldn't mind living there. Looks like a suburb, not a section of a busy borough in a busy city."

There are private homes on the street, an apartment house with the fake-Tudor front that used to be the quintessence of swank in Queens, and neigh-

18

borhood stores—a barbershop, a dry cleaner, coffee shop, a grocer—all quite cheerful except for the paint-covered window of the mail-order bookstore.

With detectives, the reporter retraced the investigation, knocked on doors, asked "Why?" He began to hate the people he talked to, he says now. That night he returned to the city room and we talked. The next day he went back with a photographer to get pictures of the neighborhood. Mostly, they met closed doors that would not open, frigid looks.

"What kind of story is this?" the photographer asked Gansberg. "It doesn't fit together. Have you got me out here on some feature?"

Thursday night when the story was in hand and edited, I talked with Turner Catledge, now Managing Editor, and with Theodore Bernstein, Assistant Managing Editor, about it. I felt professional excitement quite keenly—excitement, not participation or guilt or responsibility, those came much later—and they did, too, immediately.

On March 27, *The Times* printed the following story by Gansberg, under a single-line four-column banner on the bottom of page one:

For more than half an hour thirty-eight re-   **19**

spectable, law-abiding citizens in Queens watched a killer stalk and stab a woman in three separate attacks in Kew Gardens.

Twice the sound of their voices and the sudden glow of their bedroom lights interrupted him and frightened him off. Each time he returned, sought her out and stabbed her again. Not one person telephoned the police during the assault; one witness called after the woman was dead.

That was two weeks ago today. But Assistant Chief Inspector Frederick M. Lussen, in charge of the borough's detectives and a veteran of twenty-five years of homicide investigations, is still shocked.

He can give a matter-of-fact recitation of many

murders. But the Kew Gardens slaying baffles him—not because it is a murder, but because the "good people" failed to call the police.

"As we have reconstructed the crime," he said, "the assailant had three chances to kill this woman during a thirty-five-minute period. He returned twice to complete the job. If we had been called when he first attacked, the woman might not be dead now."

This is what the police say happened beginning at 3:20 A.M. in the staid, middle-class, tree-lined Austin Street area:

Twenty-eight-year-old Catherine Genovese, who was called Kitty by almost everyone in the neighborhood, was returning home from her job as manager of a bar in Hollis. She parked her red Fiat in a lot adjacent to the Kew Gardens Long Island Rail Road Station, facing Mowbray Place. Like many residents of the neighborhood, she had parked there day after day since her arrival from Connecticut a year ago, although the railroad frowns on the practice.

She turned off the lights of her car, locked the door and started to walk the 100 feet to the entrance of her apartment at 82-70 Austin Street, which is in a Tudor building, with stores on the first floor and apartments on the second.

The entrance to the apartment is in the rear of the building because the front is rented to retail stores. At night the quiet neighborhood is shrouded in the slumbering darkness that marks most residential areas.

Miss Genovese noticed a man at the far end of the lot, near a seven-story apartment house at 82-40 Austin Street. She halted. Then, nervously, she headed up Austin Street toward Lefferts Boulevard, where there is a call box to the 102d Police Precinct in nearby Richmond Hill.

She got as far as a street light in front of a bookstore before the man grabbed her. She screamed. Lights went on in the ten-story apartment house at 82-67 Austin Street, which faces the bookstore. Windows slid open and voices punctured the early-morning stillness.

Miss Genovese screamed: "Oh, my God, he stabbed me! Please help me! Please help me!"

From one of the upper windows in the apartment house, a man called down: "Let that girl alone!"

The assailant looked up at him, shrugged and

SERVICE
HI.1-1222
INC.
TRANSISTOR RADIOS
·HI·FI·
STEREO
REPAIRS
T.V.
HIT RECORDS!
BRAND NEW!
45 RPM's
39¢
EACH
SALE

Austin Street, Kew Gardens, where Catherine Genovese was first attacked in front of the bookstore.

walked down Austin Street toward a white sedan parked a short distance away. Miss Genovese struggled to her feet.

Lights went out. The killer returned to Miss Genovese, now trying to make her way around the side of the building by the parking lot to get to her apartment. The assailant stabbed her again.

"I'm dying!" she shrieked. "I'm dying!"

Windows were opened again, and lights went on in many apartments. The assailant got into his car and drove away. Miss Genovese staggered to her feet. A city bus, Q-10, the Lefferts Boulevard line to Kennedy International Airport, passed. It was 3:35 A.M.

The assailant returned. By then, Miss Genovese had crawled to the back of the building, where the freshly painted brown doors to the apartment house held out hope of safety. The killer tried the first door; she wasn't there. At the second door, 82-62 Austin Street, he saw her slumped on the floor at the foot of the stairs. He stabbed her a third time —fatally.

It was 3:50 by the time the police received their first call from a man who was a neighbor of Miss Genovese. In two minutes they were at the scene.

The neighbor, a seventy-year-old woman and another woman were the only persons on the street. Nobody else came forward.

The man explained that he had called the police after much deliberation. He had phoned a friend in Nassau County for advice and then he had crossed the roof of the building to the apartment of the elderly woman to get her to make the call.

"I didn't want to get involved," he sheepishly told the police.

Six days later, the police arrested Winston Moseley, a twenty-nine-year-old business-machine operator, and charged him with the homicide. Moseley had no previous record. He is married, has two children and owns a home at 133-19 Sutter Avenue, South Ozone Park, Queens. On Wednesday, a court committed him to Kings County Hospital for psychiatric observation.

When questioned by the police, Moseley also said that he had slain Mrs. Annie May Johnson, twenty-four, of 146-12 133d Avenue, Jamaica, on February 29 and Barbara Kralik, fifteen, of 174-17 140th Avenue, Springfield Gardens, last July. In the Kralik case, the police are holding Alvin L. Mitchell, who is said to have confessed that slaying.

27

Miss Genovese was stabbed a second time before the drugstore at the corner of the railroad station and parking lot.

The police stressed how simple it would have been to have gotten in touch with them. "A phone call," said one of the detectives, "would have done it." The police may be reached by dialing "O" for operator or SPring 7-3100.

The question of whether the witnesses can be held legally responsible in any way for failure to report the crime was put to the Police Department's legal bureau. There, a spokesman said:

"There is no legal responsibility, with few exceptions, for any citizen to report a crime."

Under the statutes of the city, he said, a witness to a suspicious or violent death must report it to the medical examiner. Under state law, a witness cannot withhold information in a kidnapping.

Today witnesses from the neighborhood, which is made up of one-family homes in the $35,000 to $60,000 range with the exception of the two apartment houses near the railroad station, find it difficult to explain why they didn't call the police.

Lieut. Bernard Jacobs, who handled the investigation by the detectives, said:

"It is one of the better neighborhoods. There are few reports of crimes. You only get the usual

30

Miss Catherine Genovese was
attacked for the third time
at doorway (1) by a man.
She was trying to reach
home (2) at Kew Gardens. He
struck first on the opposite
side of the block.

complaints about boys playing or garbage cans being turned over."

The police said most persons had told them they had been afraid to call, but had given meaningless answers when asked what they had feared.

"We can understand the reticence of people to become involved in an area of violence," Lieutenant Jacobs said, "but where they are in their homes, near phones, why should they be afraid to call the police?"

He said his men were able to piece together what happened—and capture the suspect—because the residents furnished all the information when detectives rang doorbells during the days following the slaying.

"But why didn't someone call us that night?" he asked unbelievingly.

Witnesses—some of them unable to believe what they had allowed to happen—told a reporter why.

A housewife, knowingly if quite casually, said, "We thought it was a lover's quarrel." A husband and wife both said, "Frankly, we were afraid." They seemed aware of the fact that events might have been different. A distraught woman, wiping her hands in her apron, said, "I didn't want my husband to get involved."

One couple, now willing to talk about that night, said they heard the first screams. The husband looked thoughtfully at the bookstore where the killer first grabbed Miss Genovese.

"We went to the window to see what was happening," he said, "but the light from our bedroom made it difficult to see the street." The wife, still apprehensive, added: "I put out the light and we were able to see better."

Asked why they hadn't called the police, she shrugged and replied: "I don't know."

A man peeked out from a slight opening in the doorway to his apartment and rattled off an account of the killer's second attack. Why hadn't he called the police at the time? "I was tired," he said without emotion. "I went back to bed."

It was 4:25 A.M. when the ambulance arrived for the body of Miss Genovese. It drove off. "Then," a solemn police detective said, "the people came out."

PART TWO

It would be pleasant to be able to say now that once the story was in print my professional aloofness disappeared, and I felt a sense of personal involvement. It would be pleasant, but quite untrue.

The only reaction I had was one of professional satisfaction. We had printed a good story, we had printed it alone, TV and the other papers were chasing after us, the *Journal-American* had printed a most handsome acknowledgment of our energy and wisdom, in which we all took quite unabashed delight.

The story had no personal involvement for me at all. I realized, as we all did, that the point we were making was that the city had become a pretty grim place, a place where thirty-eight people would not lift a finger or a telephone to help a woman being attacked under their windows. How awful of them, we were saying. Of *them*.

Naturally, we had to have a follow-up. As the night the day, a follow-up comes after any good story. And the obvious thing to do is what we did—get on the telephone to a random selection of sociologists, psychologists and theologians asking them what they thought of it all, how they could explain this strange phenomenon of a story.

I am fascinated, now, by the threads that ran through the "reaction" from our professional sources, that day and in the days that followed. The reaction of almost every one of these social physicians was to admit total failure on their part to understand, or to look for a comforting bit of jargon, or to reach out for a target—metropolitan living, or fear of the police, or TV sadism.

Everybody used a word that had been in the headline in the story—apathy.

The first follow-up story summed up the professional reaction this way:

"Expressions of shock and perplexity followed the disclosure yesterday that thirty-seven witnesses to a murder in Queens had failed to report the crime to the police." (We kept confusing readers by shifting between thirty-seven and thirty-eight; the reason was that thirty-eight had witnessed the crime or heard it, but that that one man finally did put through a call after it was too late.)

Experts in human behavior, such as psychiatrists and sociologists, our story found, seemed as hard put as anyone else to explain the inaction of the witnesses. One sociologist called it "non-rational behavior."

Leo J. Zimmerman, vice-president of the Queens Bar Association, called the incident "outrageous," and said he was "profoundly shocked." Nobody, in a newspaper story is lightly, or non-profoundly, shocked. Mr. Zimmerman took pains to point out that he was not speaking on behalf of the Bar Association.

A professor at the Downstate Medical Center of New York State University said the incident "goes to the heart of whether this is a community or a jungle." He suggested that when members of a society failed to defend each other they came close to being partners in crime. Then he added that he felt the incident was "atypical" and that New York as a community could not be condemned.

A psychiatrist called the incident typical—not atypical—of middle-class groups in a city like New York. "They have a nice life and what happens in the street, the life of the city itself, is a different matter." The same psychiatrist, Dr. George Serban, said that there was a constant feeling in New York that society was unjust and that that might be the explanation.

"It's the air of all New York, the air of injustice," he said. "The feeling that you might get hurt if you act and that whatever you do, you will be the one to suffer."

Dr. Renee Claire Fox, of Barnard College's sociology department, talked of "disaster syndromes" something like that seen in victims of sudden disasters, such as tornadoes. She said that witnessing a prolonged murder under their own windows had destroyed the witnesses' feeling that the world was a rational orderly place, and as a result "it deeply shook their sense of safety and sureness." The result, she ventured, was an "affect denial" that caused them to withdraw psychologically from the event by ignoring it.

My own favorite comment came from the theologian who said that he could not understand it, that perhaps "depersonalizing" in New York had gone farther than he thought. Then he added, in monumental, total unconsciousness of irony: "Don't quote me."

40   Ever and ever, I shall treasure that theologian.

A bit of handy jargon and then—don't quote me, don't involve me. Who are all these others? Somehow, when I read that last line in the story, I felt that every point we had to make had been made.

A variety of riders rode a variety of hobby horses. Walter Arm, the Deputy Police Commissioner for Community Relations, took the opportunity to point out that the police had long been concerned with apathy in reporting crimes, and that several hundred thousand leaflets would be distributed exhorting the public to report all crimes immediately.

Some time later, a psychiatrist, Dr. Ralph S. Banay, told a symposium on violence conducted by the Medical Correctional Association that a confusion of fantasy with reality, fed by an endless stream of TV violence, was in part responsible for the fact that the witnesses to Miss Genovese's murder had turned away. "We underestimate the damage that these accumulated images do to the brain," he said. "The immediate effect can be delusional, equivalent to a sort of posthypnotic suggestion."

Dr. Banay suggested that the murderer vicariously gratified the sadistic impulses of those who witnessed it. "They were deaf, paralyzed, hypnotized with excitation," he said. "Fascinated by the drama, by the action, and yet not entirely sure that what was taking place was actually happening."

Dr. Banay, a professor of forensic psychiatry at Manhattan College, interpreted the readiness of the witnesses to admit to the police that they had failed to act as an attempt to purge their guilt through confession. "Persons with mature and well-integrated personalities would not have acted in this way," he said.

At the same meeting, Dr. Karl Menninger, the director of the Menninger Foundation in Topeka, Kansas, touched on the same theme when he said that "public apathy is itself a manifestation of aggressiveness."

None of this sort of reaction was at all surprising. As a matter of fact, it was fairly pat and standard journalistically, and in my own mind I did not feel, nor do I now, that the sociologists and psychiatrists who commented contributed anything substantial to anybody's understanding of what happened that night on Austin Street.

I am not really sure, to this moment, just when my own attitudes toward the story began to become a little more complicated, just when I came to think of it as something perhaps a little different from another strange story of the city, began to relate it to myself and to everybody around me. Even now, as I write this, I find it difficult to make a clean and totally honest distinction between my interest in the story as a newspaperman and a peculiar, paradoxical feeling that there is in the tale of Catherine Genovese a revelation about the human condition so appalling to contemplate that only good can come from forcing oneself to confront the truth.

This belief was slow in growing. I do know that I became intensely interested in the reaction of people who wrote letters to the paper about the story, and the fact that people talked so often about it, could not seem to let it go.

It seemed to me that there were several patterns that ran through many of the letters. The first was terrible anger at the witnesses. These letter writers were totally unable to identify themselves with the witnesses and were full of a strange passion against them.

"I feel it is the duty of *The New York Times* to try to obtain the names of the witnesses involved and to publish the list," one woman wrote. "These people should be held up for public ridicule, since they cannot be held responsible for their inaction. . . .

"Apparently these thirty-seven people feel no moral obligation to their fellow men. Therefore constant reminders in the newspapers are necessary to show them the contempt in which other morally responsible citizens hold them."

Another woman, the wife of a professor, wrote: "The implications of their silence—and of the cowardice and indifference it revealed—are staggering. If the laws of New York State do not prescribe some form of punishment, then we believe your newspaper should pressure the state legislature for an amendment to those laws. And since these people did not even choose to recognize their moral responsibility we feel it would be appropriate, as a form of censure, for *The Times* to publish, preferably on page 1, the names and addresses of all thirty-seven people involved. Something must be done, and quickly, to discourage other people from such behavior in the future."

It is an open matter for endless discussion among newspapermen as to whether people who write letters represent any meaningful consensus. Many of us feel that letter writers are usually unrepresentative, that few people feel strongly enough about things to write to newspapers, and that those who do represent nothing but their own emotions. I believe that in the case of the Austin Street murder this is a little oversophisticated.

I believe this because most of the emotions I found in the letters I found in my own friends and relatives. At first, there was a shadow of individual guilt. A friend said, "Dear God, what have we come to?" and the word "we" stuck in my mind. But generally, among my friends there was more "they" than "we," particularly as the days went on. The story seemed to stick in the minds of people, to irritate them more, I think, than any in which I ever have had a part. "What kind of animals live on that street?" a friend asked me, and when I seemed startled at his vehemence he got even angrier. "Do you think this kind of behavior is normal?"

I didn't, of course, but in my mind something was bothering me—a feeling that the story had turned into a hunt for a target, and the queasy belief that the target was in our own mirrors.

But to my amazement the favorite target by far was the police. Everybody had at them, at first. An editor on *The Times,* a thoughtful man, became tight-jawed with rage when the story was discussed, **45** furious not at the people on Austin Street or what it showed about them or other people, but because he had convinced himself that the kernel of truth in the story was that New Yorkers had learned to be afraid of the police or contemptuous of them.

Judging by much of the mail, he had a good point.

"Have you ever reported anything to the police?" a letter writer demanded. "If you did, you would know that you are subjected to insults and abuse from annoyed undutiful police such as 'why don't you move out of the area' or 'why bother us, this is a bad area' or you will have a call answered 45 min. after it was put in for aid; when you show interest in law violation being told to mind own business, or go away, take a walk." Another: "Call the police! Are you kidding? . . . If you see how they operate you die laughing, funnier than the clown in the circus . . . I like everybody else sign no name I like to stay in business." Another: "Nothing annoys a precinct desk captain more than a call after ten o'clock, if you want to complain your neighbors are having a rowdy party and keeping you awake."

46   From the East Twenties in New York: "Shortly

after moving in I heard screaming on the street several times, called the police and was politely told to mind my own business."

It seemed to us that the Genovese story had become entwined with the story of public reaction to the police and the story of police operations. We took a look at the problem of patrolling and calling for help and found some interesting things. Radio cars and patrolmen are supposed to be patrolling every section of the five boroughs day and night. But as an official of the department said, "It's nice if you are at the right spot at the right time. But it isn't always possible."

The Times reported: "Part of the problem with radio cars, for example, may be attributed to traffic congestion in the areas they are covering.

"The city's 800 emergency service vehicles and radio motor patrol cars are under the jurisdiction of precinct captains in the five boroughs. There are eighty precincts.

"Cars cruise for eight hours on assignment from their precincts. Each car has a driver and a recorder, and they are expected to telephone their precincts every hour. They are under Police Headquarters orders only when the Communications Bureau assigns them to an emergency call in their area."

But in other American cities this operation is simpler. Reports from *Times* correspondents in Chicago and Atlanta showed that in those cities only one man was assigned to a patrol car, and police reported that this increased their coverage.

In Chicago, the police say they are able to use 1,400 cars at peak periods as the result of one-man operation. They can send cars to emergencies quicker because each car is assigned to a specific area.

In New York, a spot check of precincts found that the average patrol car returned to a given spot about once every forty-five minutes. A patrolman is supposed to return to certain spots every half hour and to vary his rounds to confuse people given to keeping too close an eye on police whereabouts, but in many neighborhoods, according to residents, only a fool would be fooled.

We also looked into the three most frequent complaints to find out how they were being handled in other parts of the country. The complaints were:

The difficulty of getting a call through to the Police Department.

The necessity of having to answer personal questions before action was taken.

The length of time it took police to respond to calls.

On April 6, *The Times* reported:

This sort of criticism has been overcome in other cities because municipal leaders have striven for simplicity in their police operations. All of the cities surveyed use one telephone number for emergency calls to the police. Most of them act while an officer is still taking the call.

Philadelphia, Atlanta and San Francisco have developed direct lines to their radio rooms, which dispatch cars immediately to the scene of emergency reports.

New York City's Police Commissioner, Michael J. Murphy, says that the system of separate exchanges and numbers in the five boroughs complicates the handling of emergency calls. He has assigned Capt. William J. Kanz, who is in charge of the Communications Bureau, to work out a better system with the New York Telephone Company.

A New Yorker who needs the help of the police can dial the operator or call the department number in his borough. But the borough numbers sometimes pose a problem. For example, the telephone for Staten Island is SAint George 7-1200. Yet the Police Department Official Roster issued last January 3 gives the exchange as ST George.

Persons who dial ST to reach the police on Staten Island find they are in touch with a business concern in Manhattan.

This couldn't happen in Chicago. There, all calls from citizens are placed to a common number, POlice 5-1313. Other cities also have devised single numbers that ring directly in their police headquarters.

Another delay in New York results from the fact that policemen who handle incoming calls at the Communications Bureau usually ask for identification and other details before passing the information along to a radio room for relay to a radio car in the area.

In Cincinnati this delay has been eliminated. When the police receive an emergency call from a citizen, one man takes the information while another dispatches a car. In some cases the police are on the scene before the call is completed.

The operation of each communications unit also is important to the speed with which the police can answer emergency calls. In New York there are seven such bureaus: Manhattan South and North, Brooklyn South and North and one each in the Bronx, Queens and Staten Island.

None of the other cities surveyed has such a massive structure for communications. All eleven cities have managed to centralize their units, so that directions to the police in the field can be given out simply and swiftly.

Following are reports of how other cities cope with emergency calls from the public:

BOSTON. All emergency calls go to a switchboard at Police Headquarters, with direct access to radio patrol cars. Calls are recorded on disks, which are kept for later reference. Depending on traffic conditions, the police car usually is on the scene in three or four minutes.

This city has an unusual service in relaying calls from car to car. Some patrol cars have radio equipment that makes it possible to get in touch with another car without having to go through headquarters.

Complaints that the police ask too many questions usually come from neighborhoods with lower

51

intellectual and economic levels. But the police act so quickly that they recently were able to prevent the stabbing of a man by a deranged woman in the Roxbury District.

PHILADELPHIA. A resident who dials the police telephone number is put in immediate touch with the radio room at City Hall. There are no "middle men" in the operation here, and the call is flashed to the nearest police car.

All emergency calls are recorded on pre-punched, pre-numbered IBM cards. The cards are put on a conveyor belt that carries the information to one of three radio frequencies, labeled A, B and C. From this source, a police dispatcher flashes the information on the air.

"We keep questions at a minimum," a spokesman for the police said. "Some persons are so excited, they even forget their names. We honor any kind of a call, even if it is anonymous."

ATLANTA. Persons reporting crimes here use a central number manned by three operators on fifteen incoming lines. The operators send the information to the radio room by an electronic process.

"We get disturbed if it takes more than five minutes to answer an emergency call," Superintendent of Police Fred Beerman said.

The department maintains that it can offer fast response to emergency calls because it has no precinct system. It also has changed the manning of its patrol cars. Formerly two men rode in each car; now one handles it. This, a police official said, has enabled Atlanta to spread patrol cars better.

LOUISVILLE. Emergency telephone calls are handled by a complaint desk at Police Headquarters. A printed card is filled out and passed by conveyor belt to the radio dispatcher. His instructions to the patrol car and the response are recorded on a disk.

The police do not ask for identification of the caller and do not ignore anonymous calls.

MIAMI. An emergency telephone call to the police is handled by a complaint desk, which dispatches a radio car to the scene immediately. Officials declare that the police arrive on the scene two minutes after receipt of a call.

All calls and replies are tape-recorded.

In the case of anonymous calls or instances

where people forget to give the location of the emergency, patrol cars are alerted to search their areas for trouble.

CINCINNATI. The police receive emergency calls directly. While one officer talks to the person calling, another dispatches a radio car to the scene. All calls are recorded on tape.

Failure of the public to call the police when noting a crime has been something of a problem. Officers point out that last week a holdup could have been prevented if a witness had called. He had watched a suspicious-looking man prowl in the area earlier in the day.

A woman complained recently: "Why don't you stop talking and send the police?" She didn't realize that a patrol car was already there, dispatched while she was calling.

CLEVELAND. A call to the police emergency telephone number is answered by a dispatcher in the radio room. The information is relayed directly by radio to cars cruising the city.

This system led last week to the capture of three men as they were holding up a supermarket.

A neighbor phoned the police when she saw suspicious movements in the store.

However, there have been some complaints about the police being slow to arrive.

The police are considering breaking their dispatching center into three or four local units to ease the heavy traffic at the current single telephone number.

CHICAGO. All emergency calls go to a common number and are channeled to a communications center at Police Headquarters.

As an officer receives the call on a telephone headset, he looks at a zone board before him and dispatches a car. Then he fills out an IBM index card with all the information about the call.

There are mostly one-man cars on beats, and more cars are running as a result.

The use of the common telephone number has eliminated all calls to district stations, except through headquarters. It has helped to speed the police response to emergency calls.

SALT LAKE CITY. Phone calls to the police go to a switchboard operator, who determines whether the situation requires the duty desk or the radio dispatcher. All calls are recorded on IBM cards. Delays take place when a call is not assessed correctly.

Uncertainty about jurisdiction between city police and the county sheriff's office has also delayed responses in some cases.

SAN FRANCISCO. A "hot-line" setup at Police Headquarters leads to fast responses to emergency calls. When a resident calls a central number he is asked if it is an emergency. If it is, his call is flashed to an eight-man radio operation and the line flashes red. These calls are relayed immediately to field units, and all conversations are taped.

The police maintain their own phone service through a division of electricity.

Lieut. Howard Ross, in charge of communications, says he can have a car at the point of the complaint within two or three minutes.

SEATTLE. A recent study here showed that the police responded in five minutes when the public called the emergency number. All calls go to a complaint department, where information is taken on a prepared form, which is sent by conveyor belt to the radio room. There a dispatcher sends a car to the scene. All conversations are taped.

Phone service has been uniformly good since the police got their own exchange a year ago. The single number covers the three major precincts and all the minor divisions.

At no time during the investigation of the murder of Catherine Genovese was any blame put on the police. This was a case where they seemed to function smoothly and blamelessly. But the attention focused on the case by the story in *The Times* brought out long-smoldering complaints against the mechanics of calling the police, and these stories did lead to some action.

There was a decision by the police not to insist on getting the names of people calling in with complaints, and Commissioner Murphy was able to push ahead a bit with a plan for getting a central number that would handle citizens' complaint calls from all over the city.

This is what happens now in New York. A person in trouble, or somebody who wants to complain to the police, can dial either O for Operator or the police number listed in the front of his borough telephone directory—a different number for each of the five boroughs.

In either case, the call is relayed to the borough Communications Bureau, where an officer takes the information down, asks the caller for his identity, and then passes on the information to the local precinct. There can be delays at any one of the points —the operator, the communications unit or the precinct.

The police said a few days after the story about the silent witnesses appeared that they would try to set up a central number, perhaps a number that would spell "For Help" or "Police" or the like. The telephone company said that having an easily remembered name-number would be of no help, because no matter how simple it was, too many people would spell it wrong. In any case, it will be a matter of years before New York has a central emergency number.

All this comment about—and usually against— the police that grew out of the Genovese story we dutifully reported, as we reported the rather harried police comment.

There is, to me, a boundless irony in the "anti-police" feeling that was stirred up, at least in the beginning, by the Genovese story. Rather, several ironies. To start with, it accomplished what the police most wanted—to rouse New Yorkers to a realization of how much police work was hampered by citizens' turning their backs, refusing to bear witness.

Most of all there was the irony inherent in the fact that the police found themselves getting dirty looks as the result of a case in which civilians had been entirely to blame, and in which the police machinery had responded perfectly. If any one of the witnesses had put in a call while Miss Genovese was being attacked, the chances are that she would have been saved, for when the call did come the police arrived within a matter of a few minutes.

I found myself in the rather strange position of defending the police to my friends and associates—defending them as the result of a case in which nobody really charged that they were at fault. Every time I pointed out that the cops were not at fault, somebody would tell me a story he had heard about a cop on a beat taking a bribe. It was ludicrously like that old joke about a Stalinist, asked about steel production in the Soviet Union, shouting at his American tormentor: "Yes, but how about the lynchings in your South?"

Anyway, a new bit of journalese was coined in the office:

"Here's an insert for our apathy story today."

"This looks like it could develop into an apathy angle."

"Slug it 'apathy'."

It happens often in the newspaper business that one unusual story seems to give birth to others of the same kind. For weeks after the first story our own paper and other newspapers printed stories about a variety of forms of public apathy—even the London bureau of *The Times* filed one about a British woman chasing a thief while onlookers did nothing but look on.

It was not that we went out deliberately and searched for other examples of apathy. What happened simply was that the problem of apathy was in the foreground of the minds of readers and reporters and editors. Stories that might have been passed over suddenly took on significance and were printed. I think that the Austin Street case, abysmally depressing though it was, did have the result of heightening public consciousness, and so do the police. As always happens, a couple of stories received prominence when they did not deserve it. One day a city editor of a competitive newspaper complained pleasantly that he had given big play to an apathy story—about witnesses to a rape—in the belief that *The Times* would play it big. We were not sure the story held up and played it small, and the city editor who spoke to me was a little puzzled.

A week or so later, I asked Gansberg to go back to the Austin Street neighborhood, to take another good look around.

"I walked up and down the same streets," Gansberg writes. "Only this time I didn't concentrate on learning about the murder. I looked at the people and the neighborhood. I wondered about the people. They were just going about their business.

"A man walked a dog; a woman was taking her youngsters to an afternoon social. The trees were still bare. I couldn't hate the neighborhood, for it was too much like my own in Passaic, New Jersey."

At the soda fountain where, a week before, Gansberg had talked to the owner and some cus- **61** tomers he was remembered. The owner gave him a malted and wouldn't let him pay. "You've done something," he said. "You've made us realize we should help each other."

A youngster at the counter put his sandwich down. "You were so right," he said. "Something has happened to this neighborhood. All of us realize we haven't been paying attention to each other."

Not everybody felt that way, though. Some were resentful of the attention paid to their neighborhood; some were confused. Some of the witnesses refused to talk. Those who did were considerably more angry than remorseful. They felt that *The Times* had hurt them. "You don't realize the danger!"

Some witnesses slammed the door in the reporter's face this time. They still did not want to "get involved."

Involved in what? Danger in the streets? They were in the safety of their houses, all of them. The police? They were all quite law-abiding. The courts? Perhaps. Of the thirty-eight, about eighteen had witnessed or heard each of the attacks; the other twenty had heard or seen one—enough to make them witnesses in court. This takes time and is a tedious business. But I do not find it in me to believe that they did not move to the telephone for fear of losing a day's pay in court.

This is a story without an end. All I know about it I have related above. Moseley is still under arrest and an innocent man in the eyes of the law. The witnesses do not wish to talk any more.

I know only one thing further: that somewhere in this story, some days after we printed it, I felt that there was a truth to be sought after, someplace, for myself if for nobody else. When *The Times Magazine* asked me to write a piece about the story, I wanted to eagerly, more eagerly than almost any other article I have written.

In the back of my mind, perhaps—I am not sure—was the feeling that there was, that there must be some connection between the story of the witnesses silent in the face of greater crimes—the degradation of a race, children hungering.

I am not sure, but I think there is. But in any case, I do know that I did not want to write the article to make any great political points. I think I wrote it simply for catharsis.

It happens from time to time in New York that the life of the city is frozen by an instant of shock.

In that instant the people of the city are seized by the paralyzing realization that they are one, that each man is in some way a mirror of every other man. They stare at each other—or, really, into themselves—and a look quite like a flush of embarrassment passes over the face of the city. Then the instant passes and the beat resumes and the people turn away and try to explain what they have seen, or try to deny it.

The last thirty-five minutes of the young life of Miss Catherine Genovese became such a shock in the life of the city. But at the time she died, stabbed again and again by a marauder in her quiet, dark but entirely respectable street in Kew Gardens, New York hardly took note.

It was not until two weeks later that Catherine Genovese, known as Kitty, returned in death to cry the city awake. Even then it was not her life or her dying that froze the city, but the witnessing of her murder—the choking fact that thirty-eight of her neighbors had seen her stabbed or heard her cries, and that not one of them, during that hideous half-hour, had lifted the telephone in the safety of his own apartment to call the police and try to save her life. When it was over and Miss Genovese was dead and the murderer gone, one man did call—not from his own apartment but from a neighbor's, and only after he had called a friend and asked her what to do.

The day that the story of the witnessing of the death of Miss Genovese appeared in this newspaper became that frozen instant. "Thirty-eight!" people said over and over. "Thirty-eight!"

It was as if the number itself had some special meaning, and in a way, of course, it did. One person or two or even three or four witnessing a murder passively would have been the unnoticed symptom of the disease in the city's body and again would have passed unnoticed. But thirty-eight—it was like a man with a running low fever suddenly beginning to cough blood; his friends could no longer ignore his illness, nor could he turn away from himself.

At first there was, briefly, the reaction of shared guilt. Even people who were sure that they certainly would have acted differently felt it somehow. "Dear God, what have we come to?" a woman said that day. "We," not "they."

For in that instant of shock, the mirror showed quite clearly what was wrong, that the face of mankind was spotted with the disease of apathy—all mankind. But this was too frightening a thought to live with, and soon the beholders began to set boundaries for the illness, to search frantically for causes that were external and to look for the carrier.

There was a rash of metropolitan masochism. "What the devil do you expect in a town, a jungle, like this?" Sociologists and psychiatrists reached for the warm comfort of jargon—"alienation of the individual from the group," "megalopolitan societies," "the disaster syndrome."

People who came from small towns said it could never happen back home. New Yorkers, ashamed, agreed. Nobody seemed to stop to ask whether there were not perhaps various forms of apathy and whether some that exist in villages and towns do not exist in great cities.

Guilt turned into masochism, and masochism, as it often does, became a sadistic search for a target. Quite soon, the target became the police.

There is no doubt whatsoever that the police in New York have failed, to put it politely, to instill a feeling of total confidence in the population. There are great areas in this city—fine parks as well as slums—where no person in his right mind would wander of an evening or an early morning. There is no central emergency point to receive calls for help.

And a small river of letters from citizens to this newspaper testifies to the fact that patrols are often late in answering calls and that policemen on desk duty often give the bitter edge of their tongues to citizens calling for succor.

There is no doubt of these things. But to blame the police for apathy is a bit like blaming the sea wall for springing leaks. The police of this city are more efficient, more restrained and more responsive to public demands than any others the writer has encountered in a decade of traveling the world. Their faults are either mechanical or a reflection of a city where almost every act of police self-protection is assumed to be an act of police brutality, and where a night-club comedian can, as one did the other night, stand on a stage for an hour and a half and vilify the police as brutes, thieves, homosexuals, illiterates and "Gestapo agents" while the audience howls in laughter as it drinks Scotch from bootleg bottles hidden under the tables.

There are two tragedies in the story of Catherine Genovese. One is the fact that her life was taken from her, that she died in pain and horror at the age of twenty-eight. The other is that in dying she gave every human being—not just species New Yorker—

an opportunity to examine some truths about the nature of apathy, and that this has not been done.

Austin Street, where Catherine Genovese lived, is in a section of Queens known as Kew Gardens. There are two apartment buildings and the rest of the street consists of one-family homes—red brick, stucco or wood-frame. There are Jews, Catholics and Protestants, a scattering of foreign accents, middle-class incomes.

On the night of March 13, about 3 A.M., Catherine Genovese was returning to her home. She worked late as manager of a bar in Hollis, another part of Queens. She parked her car (a red Fiat) and started to walk to her death.

Lurking near the parking lot was a man. Miss Genovese saw him in the shadows, turned and walked toward a police call box. The man pursued her, stabbed her. She screamed, "Oh my God, he stabbed me! Please help me! Please help me!"

Somebody threw open a window and a man called out: "Let that girl alone!" Other lights turned on, other windows were raised. The attacker got into a car and drove away. A bus passed.

The attacker drove back, got out, searched out Miss Genovese in the back of an apartment building where she had crawled for safety, stabbed her again, drove away again.

The first attack came at 3:15. The first call to the police came at 3:50. Police arrived within two minutes, they say. Miss Genovese was dead.

That night and the next morning the police combed the neighborhood looking for witnesses. They found them, thirty-eight.

Two weeks later, when this newspaper heard of the story, a reporter went knocking, door to door, asking why, why.

Through half-opened doors, they told him. Most of them were neither defiant nor terribly embarrassed nor particularly ashamed. The underlying attitude, or explanation, seemed to be fear of involvement—any kind of involvement.

"I didn't want my husband to get involved," a housewife said.

"We thought it was a lovers' quarrel," said another woman. "I went back to bed."

"I was tired," said a man.

"I don't know," said another man.

"I don't know," said still another.

"I don't know," said others.

On March 19, police arrested a twenty-nine-year-old business-machine operator named Winston Moseley and charged him with the murder of Catherine Genovese. He has confessed to killing two other women, for one of whose murders police say they have a confession from another man.

Not much is said or heard or thought in the city about Winston Moseley. In this drama, as far as the city is concerned, he appeared briefly, acted his piece, exited into the wings.

A week after the first story appeared a reporter went back to Austin Street. Now the witnesses no longer wanted to talk. They were harried, annoyed; they thought they should keep their mouths shut. "I've done enough talking," one witness said. "Oh, it's you again," said a woman witness and slammed the door.

The neighbors of the witnesses are willing to talk. Their sympathy is for the silent witnesses and the embarrassment in which they now live.

Max Heilbrunn, who runs a coffee house on Austin Street, talked about all the newspaper publicity and said his neighbors felt they were being picked on. "It isn't a bad neighborhood," he said.

And this from Frank Facciola, the owner of the neighborhood barber shop: "I resent the way these newspaper and television people have hurt us. We have wonderful people here. What happened could have happened any place. There is no question in my mind that people here now would rush out to help anyone being attacked on the street."

Then he said, "The same thing [failure to call the police] happens in other sections every day. Why make such a fuss when it happens in Kew Gardens? We are trying to forget it happened here."

A Frenchwoman in the neighborhood said, "Let's forget the whole thing. It is a quiet neighborhood, good to live in. What happened, happened."

Each individual, obviously, approaches the story of Catherine Genovese, reacts to it and veers away from it against the background of his own life and experience, and his own fears and shortcomings and rationalizations.

It seems to this writer that what happened in the apartments and houses on Austin Street was a symptom of a terrible reality in the human condition —that only under certain situations and only in response to certain reflexes or certain beliefs will a man step out of his shell toward his brother.

To say this is not to excuse, but to try to understand and in so doing perhaps eventually to extend the reflexes and beliefs and situations to include more people. To ignore it is to perpetuate myths that lead nowhere. Of these the two most futile philosophically are that apathy is a response to official ineptitude ("The cops never come on time anyway"), or that apathy is a condition only of metropolitan life.

Certainly police procedures must be improved —although in the story of Miss Genovese all indications were that, once called into action, the police machine behaved perfectly.

As far as is known, not one witness has said that he remained silent because he had had any unpleasant experience with the police. It is a pointless point; there are men who will jump into a river to rescue a drowner; there are others who will tell themselves that a police launch will be cruising by or that, if it doesn't, it should.

Nobody can say why the thirty-eight did not lift the phone while Miss Genovese was being attacked, since they cannot say themselves. It can be assumed, however, that their apathy was indeed of a big-city variety. It is almost a matter of psychological survival, if one is surrounded and pressed by millions of people, to prevent them from constantly impinging on you, and the only way to do this is to ignore them as often as possible.

Indifference to one's neighbor and his troubles is a conditioned reflex of life in New York as it is in other big cities. In every major city in which I have lived—in Tokyo and Warsaw, Vienna and Bombay —I have seen, over and over again, people walk away from accident victims. I have walked away myself.

Out-of-towners, and sometimes New Yorkers themselves, like to think that there is something special about New York's metropolitan apathy. It is special in that there are more people here than any place else in the country—and therefore more people to turn away from each other.

For decades, New York turned away from the truth that is Harlem or Bedford-Stuyvesant in Brooklyn. Everybody knew that in the Negro ghettos, men, women and children lived in filth and degradation. But the city, as a city, turned away with the metropolitan brand of apathy. This, most simply, consists of drowning the person-to-person responsibility in a wave of impersonal social action.

Committees were organized, speeches made, budgets passed to "do something" about Harlem or Bedford-Stuyvesant—to do something about the

73

communities. This dulled the reality, and still does, that the communities consist of individual people who ache and suffer in the loss of their individual prides. Housewives who contributed to the N.A.A.C.P. saw nothing wrong in going down to the daily shape-up of domestic workers in the Bronx and selecting a maid for the day after looking over the coffle to see which "girl" among the Negro matrons present looked huskiest.

Now there is an acute awareness of the problems of the Negroes in New York. But, again, it is an impersonal awareness, and more and more it is tinged with irritation at the thought that the integration movement will impinge on the daily personal life of the city.

Nor are Negroes in the city immune from apathy —toward one another or toward whites. They are apathetic toward one another's right to believe and act as they please; one man's concept of proper action is labeled with the group epithet "Uncle Tom." And, until the recent upsurge of the integration movement, there was less action taken within the Negro community to improve conditions in Harlem than there was in the all-white sections of the East Side. It has become fashionable to sneer at

74

"white liberals"—fashionable even among Negroes who for years did nothing for brothers even of their own color.

In their own sense of being wronged, some Negroes of New York have become totally apathetic to the sensitivities of all other groups. In a night club in Harlem the other night, an aspiring Negro politician, a most decent man, talked of how the Jewish shopkeepers exploited the Negroes, how he wished Negroes could "save a dollar like the Jews," totally apathetic toward the fact that Jews at the table might be as hurt as he would be if they talked in clichés of the happy-go-lucky Stepin Fetchit Negro. When a Jew protested, the Negro was stunned—because he was convinced he hated anti-Semitism. He did, in the abstract.

Since the Genovese case, New Yorkers have sought explanations of their apathy toward individuals. Fear, some say—fear of involvement, fear of reprisal from goons, fear of becoming "mixed up" with the police. This, it seems to this writer, is simply rationalization.

The self-protective shells in which we live are determined not only by the difference between big cities and small. They are determined by economics and social class, by caste and by color, and by religion, and by politics.

If I were to see a beggar starving to death in rags in the streets of Paris or New York or London I would be moved to take some kind of action. But many times I have seen starving men lying like broken dolls in the streets of Calcutta or Madras and have done nothing.

I think I would have called the police to save Miss Genovese but I know that I did not save a beggar in Calcutta. Was my failing really so much smaller than that of the people who watched from their windows on Austin Street? And what was the apathy of the people of Austin Street compared, let's say, with the apathy of non-Nazi Germans toward Jews?

Geography is a factor of apathy. Indians reacted to Portuguese imprisoning Goans, but not to Russians killing Hungarians.

Color is a factor. Ghanaians reacted toward Frenchmen killing Algerians, not toward Congolese killing white missionaries.

Strangeness is a factor. Americans react to the extermination of Jews but not to the extermination of Watusis.

76

There are national as well as individual apathies, all inhibiting the ability to react. The "mind-your-own-business" attitude is despised among individuals, and clucked at by sociologists, but glorified as pragmatic national policy among nations.

Only in scattered moments, and then in halting embarrassment, does the United States, the most involved nation in the world, get down to hard cases about the nature of governments with which it deals, and how they treat their subject citizens. People who believe that a free government should react to oppression of people in the mass by other governments are regarded as fanatics or romantics by the same diplomats who would react in horror to the oppression of one single individual in Washington. Between apathy, regarded as a moral disease, and national policy, the line is often hard to find.

There are, it seems to me, only two logical ways to look at the story of the murder of Catherine Genovese. One is the way of the neighbor on Austin Street—"Let's forget the whole thing."

The other is to recognize that the bell tolls even on each man's individual island, to recognize that every man must fear the witness in himself who whispers to close the window.

77

A. M. Rosenthal is a columnist and former executive editor of the *New York Times*. In 1960 he won a Pulitzer Prize for his reporting from Poland. As assistant managing editor, managing editor, and executive editor, Rosenthal was in charge of daily news operations for the *Times* for about sixteen years. The coauthor (with Arthur Gelb) of *One More Victim,* Rosenthal has also won several Overseas Press Club awards for his reporting from India, Pakistan, Nepal, Afghanistan, the former Ceylon, New Guinea, and Vietnam.